Polar Bears

by Marcia S. Freeman

Consulting Editor:
Gail Saunders-Smith, Ph.D.

Consultant:
Don Middleton, Member
International Association for
Bear Research and Management

Pebble Books

an imprint of Capstone Press
Mankato, Minnesota

Pebble Books are published by Capstone Press
818 North Willow Street, Mankato, Minnesota 56001
http://www.capstone-press.com

Library of Congress Cataloging-in-Publication Data
Freeman, Marcia S. (Marcia Sheehan), 1937–
  Polar bears/by Marcia S. Freeman.
      p. cm.—(Bears)
  Includes bibliographical references and index.
  Summary: Simple text and photographs introduce the appearance, behavior, and habitat of
polar bears.
  ISBN 0-7368-0099-9
  1. Polar bear—Juvenile literature. [1. Polar bear. 2. Bears.] I. Title. II. Series.
QL737.C27F7295 1999
599.786—dc21   98-19943
                                                                    CIP
                                                                    AC

Note to Parents and Teachers

Books in this series may be used together in comparative activities to investigate different types of bears. The series supports the national science education standards for units on the diversity and unity of animal life. This book describes and illustrates the appearance and activities of the polar bear. The photographs support early readers in understanding the text. The sentence structures offer subtle challenges. This book introduces early readers to vocabulary used in this subject area. The vocabulary is defined in the Words to Know section. Early readers may need assistance in reading some words and in using the Table of Contents, Words to Know, Read More, Internet Sites, and Index/Word List sections of the book.

Table of Contents

Polar bears are some of the largest bears in the world.

Polar bears live
in the Arctic.

Polar bears have thick, white fur. Fur keeps polar bears warm.

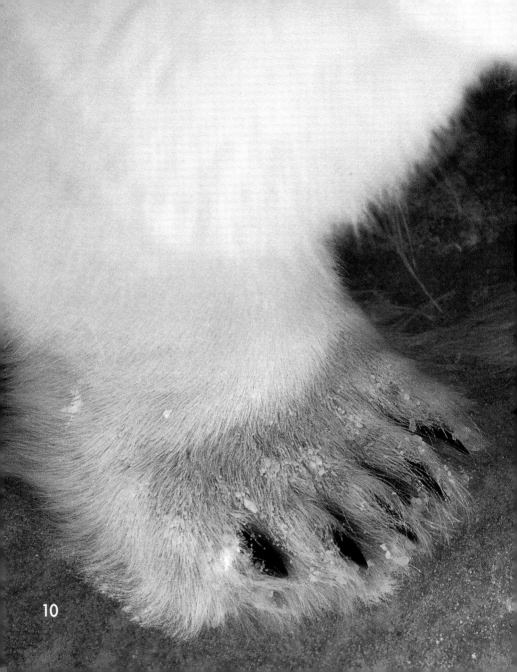

10

Polar bears have webbed toes.

Webbed toes help
polar bears swim.

Polar bears dive into icy water. They swim to ice floes to hunt for food.

Polar bears hunt seals and walrus pups.

Female polar bears
have cubs during winter.

Female polar bears teach their cubs how to hunt.

Words to Know

Arctic—the frozen area around the North Pole

cub—a young bear

female—a person or animal that can give birth or lay eggs

hunt—to chase and kill animals for food

ice floe—a sheet of floating ice

pup—a young animal; young walruses are called pups.

seal—a sea mammal that has thick fur and flippers and lives in coastal waters

walrus—a sea animal that has tusks and flippers and lives in the Arctic

webbed—connected by pieces of skin; polar bears have webbed toes.

Read More

DuTemple, Lesley A. *Polar Bears.* Early Bird Nature Books. Minneapolis: Lerner Publications, 1997.

Helmer, Diana Star. *Polar Bears.* Bears of the World. New York: PowerKids Press, 1997.

Holmes, Kevin J. *Bears.* Animals. Mankato, Minn.: Bridgestone Books, 1998.

Pfeffer, Wendy. *Polar Bears.* Creatures in White. Parsippany, N.J.: Silver Press, 1997.

Internet Sites

The Polar Bear and the Walrus
http://www.teelfamily.com/activities/polarbear/

Polar Bears
http://www.nature-net.com/bears/polar.html

Polar Bears Galore!
http://www.onu.edu/bears.html

Index/Word List

Word Count: 77
Early-Intervention Level: 9

Editorial Credits
Michelle L. Norstad, editor; Clay Schotzko/Icon Productions, cover designer;
Sheri Gosewisch, photo researcher

Photo Credits
Daniel J. Cox, 8, 10, 14
Dembinsky Photo Assoc. Inc./Mark J. Thomas, 4; Darrell Gulin, 12; E and D
Husking, 16
John Serrao, cover
Photo Network/Mark Newman, 1
Root Resources/Anthony Mercieca, 6; Claudia Adams, 18
Valan Photos/Wayne Lankinen, 20